EPIC ANIMAL
JOURNEYS

Ed J Brown

CONTENTS

WANDERING THE WORLD: AN INTRODUCTION

Migrating animals are found in all the branches of the animal kingdom – birds, fish, crustaceans, reptiles, amphibians, mammals, and insects all undertake great journeys across water, land or air. These are some of the most impressive migration record holders:

Smallest migrant	1–2 mm long	Zooplankton (see p. 50)
Largest migrant	24–27 m long	Blue whale
Longest mammal migration	Up to 8,500 km each way	Humpback whale
Longest insect migration	Up to 4,750 km each way	Monarch butterfly (see p. 38)
Longest recorded round-trip	60,000 km	Arctic tern (See p. 20)

The journeys push the animals to their very limits; they must cross difficult terrain, relying on the resources they stocked up on in the summer to last them through weeks or even months of physical effort. They often reach their destination weak, exhausted and vulnerable to predators. Many will perish along the way.

SO WHY DO IT?

The risks of migration must be outweighed by its benefits to the species as a whole. Most species migrate to feed, reproduce or both.

In the cold or the dry season, when food is scarce, animals will migrate to greener pastures. The caribou up in the Arctic Circle will travel south in the winter, living off lichen until they reach the forests of the Yukon. Wildebeest will follow the rains, so that they may feast on the lushest grasslands. Bird species fly thousands of miles from Europe to Africa, where insects and berries are plentiful.

Some animals migrate to reach their breeding grounds. Often this happens at the other end of the food migration – birds will spend their winters in the south and then nest in colder, northern climes where there are fewer predators. Whales do the reverse journey – they breed in warm, southern waters, so that their young have time to build up a layer of blubber to protect them in the icy polar seas. Some animals, like salmon and eels, will migrate only once in their lifetime, crossing vast oceans to reach the precise spot in which they were born, so that they may spawn.

Migration serves many important purposes. It allows a species to prosper by making sure that they are not overpopulating a certain area. The difficult journeys mean that only the strongest survive, keeping the genetic pool of the species fit and healthy. Migration also plays an important ecological role, keeping plant and insect life in check, whilst also allowing it time to regenerate each year.

HOW DOES IT WORK?

We now know that animals use the earth's magnetic field to guide them on their epic journeys around the planet, but there are still many mysteries left to uncover. Scientists are exploring what gives animals their incredible 'compass' sense, and how their other senses work together to help them navigate many thousands of miles across ever-changing terrain. Once we have the answer to these questions, we can better understand the effects that human activities are having on migrating animals, and how we may be able to protect them.

The incredible migrations of animals over air, land and sea remind us how the world's habitats are connected and rely on one another, and how important it is for us humans to look after this unique planet that we share with so many other species.

AIR migration

Roughly half the world's nearly 10,000 known bird species migrate, including songbirds, sea birds, raptors and waders. Some of these migrations are short, but many birds make truly epic journeys, crossing continents and oceans, with no obstacles to slow them down.

Many migration record holders belong to the avian (bird) world; the Arctic tern is the record-holder for distance, travelling 60,000 km from pole to pole and back. The great snipe reaches speeds of 80 km/h, making it the fastest, and the bar-tailed godwit flies 10,000 km in 11 days without stopping, making it the master of endurance.

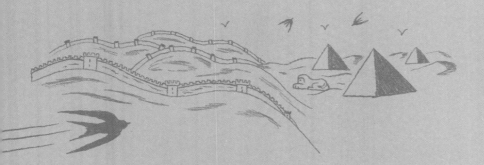

All over the world, right this very moment, millions of birds are on the move. Keep an eye out in spring and autumn as flocks of migratory birds pass overhead. Thinking about where they've come from and where they're heading can be awe-inspiring indeed.

ABOUT A BIRD

Birds are the first animals we think of when we think about migration. About half of all birds take part in annual migrations. In northern areas, like Scandinavia, almost all the bird species migrate south to avoid the winter cold. In temperate regions, about half the species migrate, and in hot regions, like the Amazon Rainforest, almost no species migrate, as the weather and food supplies are steady year-round.

Ringing is when a lightweight metal band with a unique number on it is placed on a bird's leg so that scientists can identify it.

In the past, it was not known where birds disappeared to over the winter months. Today we have a clear idea of which birds fly where and for how long. Scientists use satellite tracking, DNA testing and ringing to trace individual birds on their journeys.

Because migrating birds are reliant more than one habitat, they are particularly vulnerable to the effects of climate change and habitat loss. Understanding their journeys helps us focus our efforts to protect them.

Turtle doves are Europe's only long-distance migratory dove. They spend their summers in the south-east of England and migrate a distance of 5,000 km to winter in Senegal.

Turtle doves used to be a common British species, but their numbers have declined by 93% since 1994. By tagging and monitoring the birds, Scientists found that they were producing only half the number of chicks as they did in the 1970s. The reason for this is that, unlike other birds who eat a combination of foods, the turtle dove's diet relies entirely on seeds. As weed seeds diminish, so does the turtle dove population.

With this knowledge, conservationists can focus their efforts on establishing feeding habitats so that they can save the species from extinction.

WHY DO BIRDS MIGRATE?

Most migrating birds breed in temperate and northern climates, flying south as the insects disappear in winter months. In the summer breeding season, they return to the north, where there are fewer predators and more nesting sites.

The reverse migration pattern happens in the Southern Hemisphere; birds fly north during the colder months. However, there are smaller landmasses in the Southern Hemisphere, so fewer species make the south-north journey.

Not all bird species follow this migration pattern. Some migrate in different ways and for different reasons:

The skylark has a short migration. It flies from the highlands of Scotland in summer to the lowlands of England in winter, where it is a crucial few degrees warmer.

Shelducks migrate from England to the remote North Sea island of Heligoland in late summer, where they moult all their flight feathers. There are no predators on Heligoland, so the birds can stay safe until their new feathers have regrown.

The Atlantic puffin is an unusual case. It nests in a temperate region and then travels north in the winter to spend eight months fishing in the chilly seas around Iceland, not stepping foot on land until the following summer.

BARN SWALLOW

For many years, it was unknown where swallows
disappeared to at the end of summer. There were some theories
that they spent their winters buried in pond muck and others that they flew to
the moon. We now know that they don't travel quite as far as the moon, but they
do migrate all the way from Europe to South Africa; a journey of 10,000 km.
They fly during daylight at quite low altitudes, covering around 300 km in a day.
At night they roost in huge flocks in reed-beds that they return to each year.

Swallows eat on the wing, snapping up flies, aphids and flying ants as they travel, following the warm weather (and insects) southwards.

Their route takes them through France, along Spain, into Morocco, and then across the vast Sahara Desert, where insects are few and far between. During this part of the flight, many die of starvation and exhaustion, meaning that only the strongest survive to pass their genes onto the next generation.

When they return, the swallows often use the same nest from the previous year. A well-constructed nest means a happy marriage. A pair of swallows only splits up if a nest collapses!

MIGRATION ROUTES

The whole world is criss-crossed with bird migration routes. In Asia, many species travel from northern areas down to Indonesia or Australia for the winter. In the Americas, birds will fly from the northern USA and Canada down to Central and South America. European birds usually spend their winters in Africa.

Most bird populations travel the exact same migration route every year. These regular flight paths are called flyways. The flyways are not always the most direct route from north to south. They need to take into account refuelling stops and wind patterns. Often, the flyways follow coastlines, rivers or mountain ranges. Many flyways avoid seas and deserts, where stopping would be impossible.

Some birds choose the most direct route, no matter how challenging it may be. Pied flycatchers fly across the Sahara Desert in a 40-60 hour flight without once taking a rest.

Broad-winged birds, like storks, rely on thermal columns of rising air to allow them to soar. Thermal columns only form over land, so these birds must cross seas at their narrowest points.

Storks will gather at easy crossing points in Israel and Turkey, waiting in great numbers for the thermals that will carry them over the Mediterranean Sea to Africa.

Some bird species return to their breeding grounds via a different route. This is called loop migration.

Oceans are no barriers for waterbirds like this gannet. They are strong swimmers and their oily feathers keep them afloat, so they will often take a break on the sea to rest and snack.

PREPARING FOR THE JOURNEY

Towards the end of summer, special hormones are released in the brains of birds that tell them to prepare for their long flight. As the days get shorter, they will start eating voraciously, building up body fat for the journey. Even birds that mostly eat insects will start eating more fruits, grains and high energy seeds. They will also start growing new feathers that are capable of withstanding difficult weather and wind conditions.

For a bird that weighs 15 grams (half the weight of a lightbulb), each gram of extra body fat can power 200 km of flight.

Different birds migrate at different speeds, depending on how they get their energy. Small birds build up fat that sees them through a short, fast journey. Warblers can make it from the UK to Africa in less than three weeks.

Larger birds would become too heavy to fly if they stored up too much fat. An osprey must stop regularly for food. It also relies on thermal currents to help it along its way, so it takes over two months for an osprey to travel a similar distance to the warbler.

Ospreys were once extinct in the British Isles, but were reintroduced 30 years ago and are now thriving. Chicks make the journey to Africa at the tender age of 12 weeks. The male osprey will stay with them until the smallest is ready to depart, but the chicks make the journey on their own. Only half will survive.

MODES OF TRANSPORT

How a bird flies can tell us a lot about how quickly it will get to where it's going and how much energy it needs to get there. Migrating birds fall into two categories; the gliders and the flappers.

Royal Tern

Golden Eagle

THE GLIDERS

Birds like eagles, hawks and terns have large wings compared to their body size. This allows them to take advantage of warm air currents called 'thermals'. Thermal currents occur when the sun heats the ground and the ground heats the air directly above it.

Albatross

Peregrine Falcon

This creates a spiral of air that pushes upwards. Gliding birds circle upwards on a thermal, soar for a distance, and then lose height until they reach the next thermal current. Thermals only happen during daytime hours, so gliders cannot fly at night.

Gliding is a very energy efficient mode of travel, saving 75-95% of the energy used by flapping flight (see p. 22). This means that gliders spend less time refuelling on the ground, which can make their journey time quicker, but they are reliant on finding the next thermal, so their route is often less direct. With the right wind conditions and thermal currents, gliders can easily cover 1,000 km in one day.

A bar-tailed godwit has been recorded migrating from Alaska to New Zealand, a distance of almost 11,000 km, in just six days!

ARCTIC TERN

The Arctic tern is a glider that holds the long-distance migration record for birds. It travels from its breeding ground in the Arctic Circle, all the way down to Antarctica and then returns, enjoying two summers and experiencing the most daylight of any animal species.

Terns live in colonies, which migrate together. Just before they set off on their epic journey, the normally noisy colony falls silent. This behaviour is called dread. After dread they take to the air all at once.

Arctic terns take a very indirect route to their destinations, often zig-zagging hundreds of miles out of the way to make the most of good weather conditions, strong thermal currents or a plentiful food source.

As a result, they cover a distance greater than the circumference of the earth each year; around 60,000 km. Over the course of its 30-year lifespan, an Arctic tern will travel the equivalent distance of five return trips to the moon!

COMMON SWIFT

Swifts belong to a family of birds called *apodidae*, which literally means 'without feet', as these little birds' feet barely ever touch the ground. They eat, court, feed and even sleep on the fly, spending about ten months of the year in the air.

Swifts are versatile flyers. The shape of their wings can adapt to different tasks, folding back to chase insects or stretching out to sleep in flight. Whilst they are expert gliders, they will also flap to propel themselves faster.

Swifts will cover up to 800 km per day, refuelling as they fly. Even at speeds of 70 km/h, swifts can discern between different types of bugs, skilfully picking out only the most delicious ones.

Birds like ducks, geese and swans have relatively small wings for their body size and they must flap continuously in order to maintain flight. This uses lots of energy and they need to make frequent stops to rest and to eat along their journey.

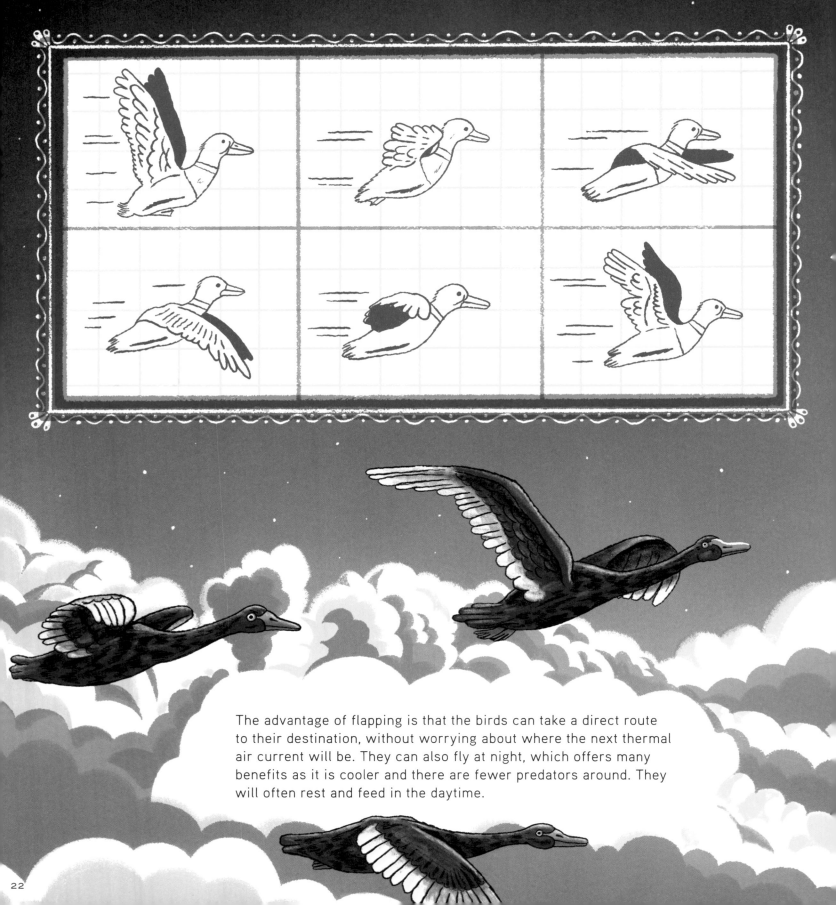

The advantage of flapping is that the birds can take a direct route to their destination, without worrying about where the next thermal air current will be. They can also fly at night, which offers many benefits as it is cooler and there are fewer predators around. They will often rest and feed in the daytime.

Gliders are restrained by the height of thermals, but flappers can fly at high altitudes. This is why it is hard to see many small migrating birds; they usually fly too high to see from the ground.

Ducks and geese are fast, heavy birds, using powerful wing beats to fly at speeds of over 40 km/h. There is less wind resistance at high altitudes, so they can fly more efficiently.

BOUNDING FLIGHT

Some small migratory birds, like finches, fly in an undulating (wavy) pattern called 'bounding flight'. They flap a few times, then close their wings to reduce air resistance and dip down. This allows them to fly longer distances, faster, saving about 10-15% of their energy. It's a bit like pedalling your bike fast and then coasting before you pedal again.

FLOCKS AND FORMATIONS

Birds often migrate in flocks, as each individual bird in a group is less likely to be attacked by a predator than if it were travelling alone.

Many large flapping birds, like geese, fly in a V-formation. The bird at the front of the V breaks up the wall of air that the flock flies into. This creates an air pocket which gives a lift to the next bird behind. Each bird in the V flies slightly higher up than the bird in front of them, maximising the extra lift of air.

V-formation is also known as the 'drafting effect'.

Flying in formation saves a whopping 70% of energy, allowing the birds to cover greater distances than they would in solo flight. The group maintains communication by calling to one another as they fly, keeping an eye on any laggers falling behind.

The bird at the front is doing most of the hard work, so after a while, she will drop back and another experienced flyer will take over.

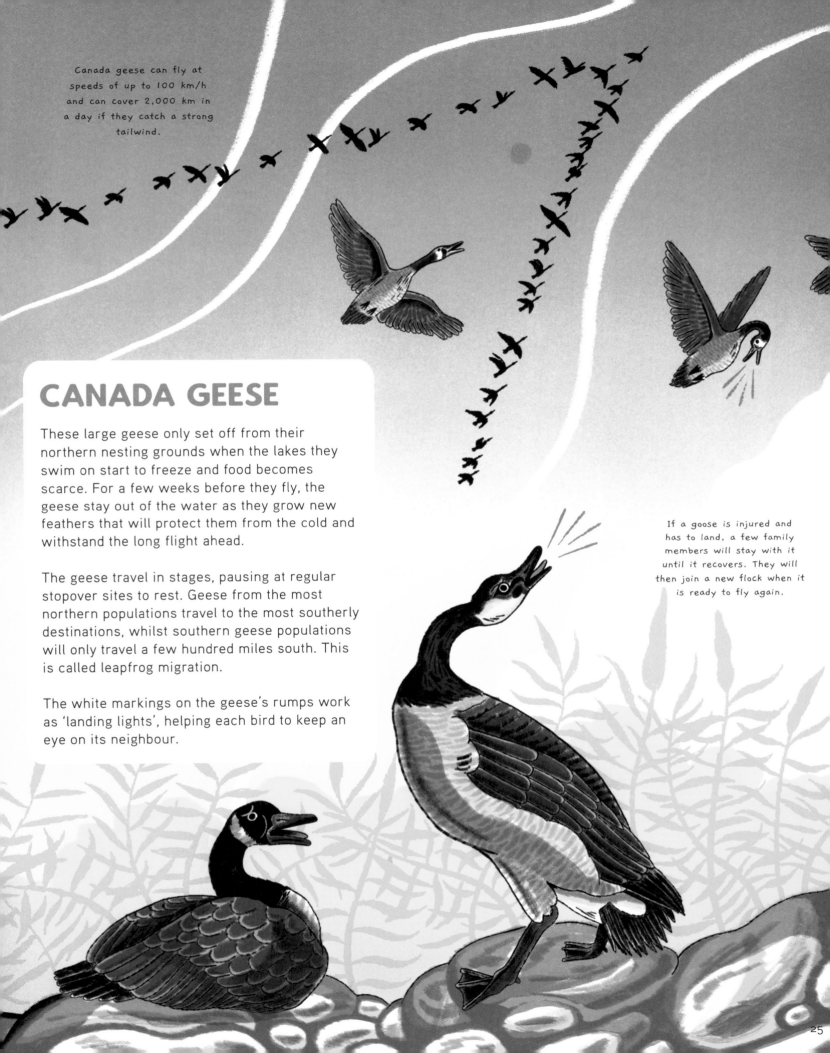

Canada geese can fly at speeds of up to 100 km/h and can cover 2,000 km in a day if they catch a strong tailwind.

CANADA GEESE

These large geese only set off from their northern nesting grounds when the lakes they swim on start to freeze and food becomes scarce. For a few weeks before they fly, the geese stay out of the water as they grow new feathers that will protect them from the cold and withstand the long flight ahead.

The geese travel in stages, pausing at regular stopover sites to rest. Geese from the most northern populations travel to the most southerly destinations, whilst southern geese populations will only travel a few hundred miles south. This is called leapfrog migration.

The white markings on the geese's rumps work as 'landing lights', helping each bird to keep an eye on its neighbour.

If a goose is injured and has to land, a few family members will stay with it until it recovers. They will then join a new flock when it is ready to fly again.

THE GREAT SNIPE

This plump little wading bird doesn't look like much, but it is the fastest long-distance flapper in the world. During its annual migration from northern Sweden to Sub-Saharan Africa, it covers a distance of 6,800 km at speeds of about 100 km/h.

It can fly for 96 hours at a stretch, taking almost no breaks and completing its migration in only four days. By the time it reaches its destination, it will have lost half its body weight.

Researchers found that the snipe tends to fly at very high altitudes of over 7,000 m in daylight hours, sinking to lower altitudes in the evening. This is because it flaps its wings seven times per second, generating a lot of body heat. Flying at higher, cooler altitudes keeps the little bird from overheating.

LAYOVER FLIGHT

Not all migrating birds have the stamina of the great snipe. Most will make several stops to recoup their strength along the way. Areas where many birds gather to rest and refuel during a migration are called 'stopover sites,' and some of them can attract vast numbers.

Hawk Mountain in Pennsylvania draws around 3,000 soaring raptors per day during their autumn migration.

The coast of Jiangsu Province in China is an important stopover site for two highly endangered little shorebirds; the spoon-billed sandpiper and the Nordmann's greenshank. They spend up to three months here gobbling up seafood and replacing their feathers on their journey from Russia to Southeast Asia.

LAND
migration

Migrations over land are often shorter than air migrations, but no less dramatic. Whilst a lot of land animals hibernate through the winter, migratory land mammals, insects and reptiles make seasonal journeys in order to find vegetation and escape harsh weather. The American bison, for example, moves slowly and steadily throughout the year, following the sun and travelling about 3 km a day. This is called 'nomadic migration'.

Other land animals migrate in search of mates. Male African elephants journey southwards in herds in search of female herds to mate with. Toads will travel a short but treacherous journey in order to reach their spawning ponds.

Without the freedom of flight, these animals must negotiate a constantly changing landscape. Roads, fences and buildings have altered the face of the natural environment, placing physical barriers in the paths of old migration routes. Challenging terrain, extreme weather conditions and the constant threat of predators mean that only the strongest of a species will make it through.

LARGE MAMMALS

Most large migratory land mammals are herbivores, or plant eaters, belonging to a mammalian order called *artiodactyla*. These animals have cloven hooves, meaning their hooves are divided into two toes.

Wildebeests, gazelles, giraffes and caribou are all migratory mammals that belong to the artiodactyla family. Zebras are literally the odd one out, as they have only one toe. They belong to the same family as tapirs and rhinoceroses.

An easy way to tell if an animal has a cloven hoof is if it has horns. Only animals with cloven hooves have horns or antlers.

These herbivores need plenty of vegetation to nourish their large bodies. A zebra, for example, will spend more than 19 hours a day grazing. Because they graze with their heads down, they are vulnerable to predators. They move in large herds, finding safety in numbers and taking turns eating and looking out for predators.

Big herds of large mammals require literally tons of fresh vegetation to sustain them. They must therefore constantly move, following plant growth and the rains that cause the vegetation to flourish.

Migration is not just vital for the survival of the animals but also for the ecosystems they inhabit. Plant growth is kept in check, keeping the soil healthy, and there is time for the vegetation to grow back once the herd has moved on.

No carnivorous land mammals migrate, although predators often follow herds of herbivores, especially if food is scarce in their home territory.

THE GREAT MIGRATION OF THE SERENGETI

August
September
July
October
November
May
June
December
April
March
January
February

The migration of millions of animals across the East African savannah is a moving spectacle. Each year, 1.5 million wildebeest, 200,000 zebra and 300,000 gazelles follow the rains north from Tanzania to Kenya and back in a journey of over 1,500 km.

Savannah is a vast, grassy plain with scattered trees.

Although the migration is continuous, it 'begins' in February on the fertile southern plains of the Ngorongoro Conservation Area. This part of the Serengeti has lush grasslands fed by rich volcanic soil. Over a million wildebeest gather to give birth to around 400,000 calves over a four-week period.

In March, when the water and grass begin to dry up, the wildebeest (and other animals) start to move north, splitting into smaller herds of a few hundred animals.

In July, the herds gather once more for the crossing of the great Mara River. Hordes of wildebeest urgently stampede across the dangerous waters. Many are crushed in the frenzy, and many others are devoured by the giant crocodiles that infest the river. Those that do make it to the other side must avoid the big cats, hyenas and other predators lying in wait.

The animals strong enough to survive this ordeal then make their way to Kenya's Maasai Mara National Reserve, where they spend a couple of months grazing before heading back to their breeding grounds around October.

CARIBOU

The land mammal with the longest migration route is the caribou, a type of reindeer found in the Arctic climes of North America. Each year they travel a round trip journey of almost 5,000 km.

Caribou are taller and lankier than their European reindeer cousins. They have larger hooves that spread their weight and support them on the snow.

The underside of the hoof has a scoop shape, good for digging through the snow for food.

The largest caribou herd is the Porcupine herd of Alaska (named for the Porcupine River, which they migrate along). Numbering around 220,000, this herd will begin its long journey south when the first snows fall, around September or October.

Caribou are the only member of the deer family in which both the males and the females grow antlers.

As they travel, plant growth becomes scarce and the caribou must eat lichen, a crusty, hard-to-digest plant that grows on rocks and trees and which can survive the cold.

They winter in the forests of northern Ontario and Quebec, beginning their return journey in March. They will birth their young in May on the remote Arctic coastal plain, where predators are few and far between.

SMALL MAMMALS

Smaller mammals tend to hibernate rather than migrate in the winter, as they cannot travel the long distances required to escape the cold. The few small mammals that migrate do so for different reasons and in rather unusual ways...

LEMMINGS

This small Scandinavian rodent lives in burrows in the Arctic tundra. In warmer years, when food is plentiful, lemmings breed very fast. Each female has four to nine babies, and after four weeks, those babies have litters of their own.

This means that in certain years, when the winter has been short and mild, the lemmings experience a population explosion. Suddenly, there is not enough food and water to support them, and they begin to move simultaneously in a mass across the countryside.

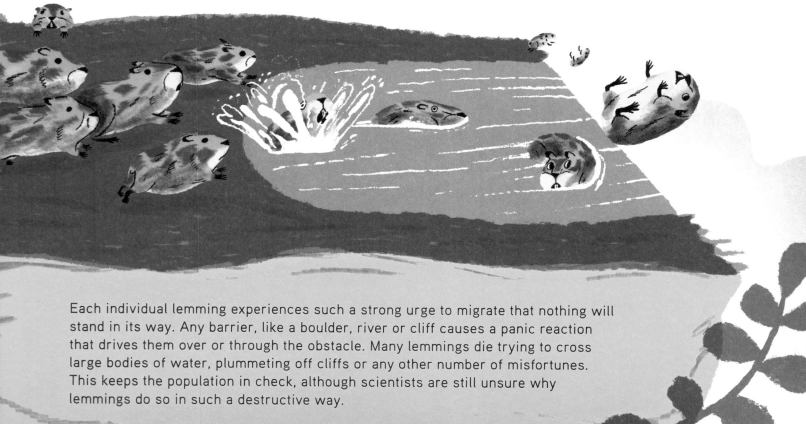

Each individual lemming experiences such a strong urge to migrate that nothing will stand in its way. Any barrier, like a boulder, river or cliff causes a panic reaction that drives them over or through the obstacle. Many lemmings die trying to cross large bodies of water, plummeting off cliffs or any other number of misfortunes. This keeps the population in check, although scientists are still unsure why lemmings do so in such a destructive way.

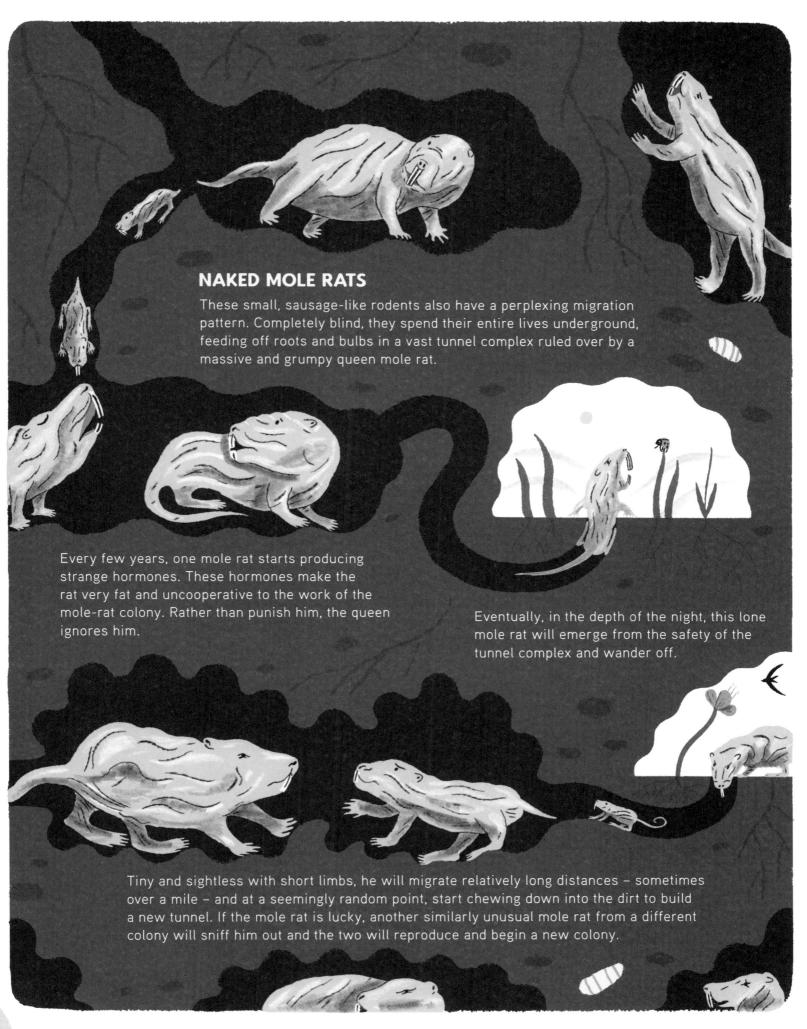

NAKED MOLE RATS

These small, sausage-like rodents also have a perplexing migration pattern. Completely blind, they spend their entire lives underground, feeding off roots and bulbs in a vast tunnel complex ruled over by a massive and grumpy queen mole rat.

Every few years, one mole rat starts producing strange hormones. These hormones make the rat very fat and uncooperative to the work of the mole-rat colony. Rather than punish him, the queen ignores him.

Eventually, in the depth of the night, this lone mole rat will emerge from the safety of the tunnel complex and wander off.

Tiny and sightless with short limbs, he will migrate relatively long distances – sometimes over a mile – and at a seemingly random point, start chewing down into the dirt to build a new tunnel. If the mole rat is lucky, another similarly unusual mole rat from a different colony will sniff him out and the two will reproduce and begin a new colony.

INSECTS

Insect species migrate in different ways – wingless insects will travel a few metres, whilst winged insects can undertake bigger journeys. African locusts travel over 100 km in a day in giant swarms, devouring all vegetation that lies in their way. Dragonflies hold the record for long-distance insect migration, catching tailwinds to travel from India to Africa. Ladybirds have shorter migrations from lowlands in the summer to mountains in the winter.

Many migratory insects, including aphids, grasshoppers and butterflies have polymorphic forms. This means that members of the same species can have different body types depending on whether they are responsible for mating or migrating.

MONARCH BUTTERFLIES

Monarch butterflies are the most famous insect migrants. They spend the winters on a small mountain range in the middle of Mexico, huddling together in their millions in the branches of fir trees.

When spring comes, the butterflies will start making their way north. Their lifecycle is just five to seven weeks. At various points in the journey, they will stop and lay their eggs on milkweed plants, dying shortly after doing so.

Milkweed contains a substance that is poisonous to most animals, making the monarch butterfly an unappetising snack for predators.

The eggs hatch into caterpillars, which within a week form a chrysalis. Adult butterflies emerge soon after and continue the journey north. It takes four or five generations of butterflies to complete the migration to their summer home in the northeastern USA and Canada.

When autumn comes, the monarchs head back to Mexico. However, the butterflies that make the return journey look and behave differently to the ones that made the journey north. They are bigger, with longer wings and darker colouring. They live for eight months, making the whole 7,500 km journey south in a single generation.

Like gliding birds, monarch butterflies take advantage of air currents to help them on their epic journey.

REPTILES & AMPHIBIANS

Reptiles and amphibians are perfectly adapted to their immediate environment and tend not to migrate, instead slowing down their body functions when the weather gets cold. Migration in these animals tends to be short distances to and from egg-laying sites.

The average life span of a giant tortoise is over 100 years. The oldest known tortoise was 176 years old.

GIANT TORTOISES

The huge tortoises of the Galapagos live in the humid highlands of the island, where there is plenty of food. In the wet season, they trek across the volcanic slopes down to the dry zone. The 250 kg reptiles move very slowly indeed. Although they only cover a distance of six or seven kilometres, the journey can take almost three weeks. The tortoises lay their eggs in the dry lowland before making the leisurely journey back.

TOADS

Every spring, toads across Britain and Europe come out of hibernation and make their way to the pond in which they were born so that they can breed. Thousands of toads travel along the same migration routes every year, covering distances of up to two kilometres.

Unlike frogs, which leap with their strong back legs, toads crawl, so the journey is slow and arduous; a single road crossing can take 15 minutes. Toads migrate at night, when their delicate skin is less likely to dry out. This makes them harder to see, and in the UK alone, 20 tonnes of toads are killed on the roads each year.

SEA migration

Oceans cover 70% of our planet and contain over 32,000 species of fish alone – that's more than the total of all other vertebrate species (amphibians, reptiles, birds and mammals) combined.

Because we can't easily see what is happening beneath the surface of the ocean, there is still much we don't know about the migration patterns of marine animals. What we do know is that great journeys are happening all the time. Fish, turtles, crustaceans, sea mammals and even micro-organisms like plankton all migrate; sometimes crossing entire oceans and sometimes travelling from the darkest depths of the seas to the surface.

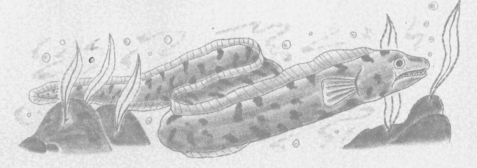

As the oceans warm due to climate change, marine animals are having to change their behaviour patterns much more quickly than other animals. Cold-blooded animals can only tolerate a narrow range of temperatures, so many species are moving to cooler waters. This changes marine ecosystems in ways that we still do not fully understand.

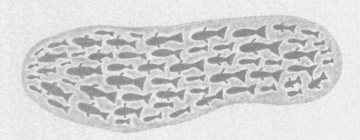

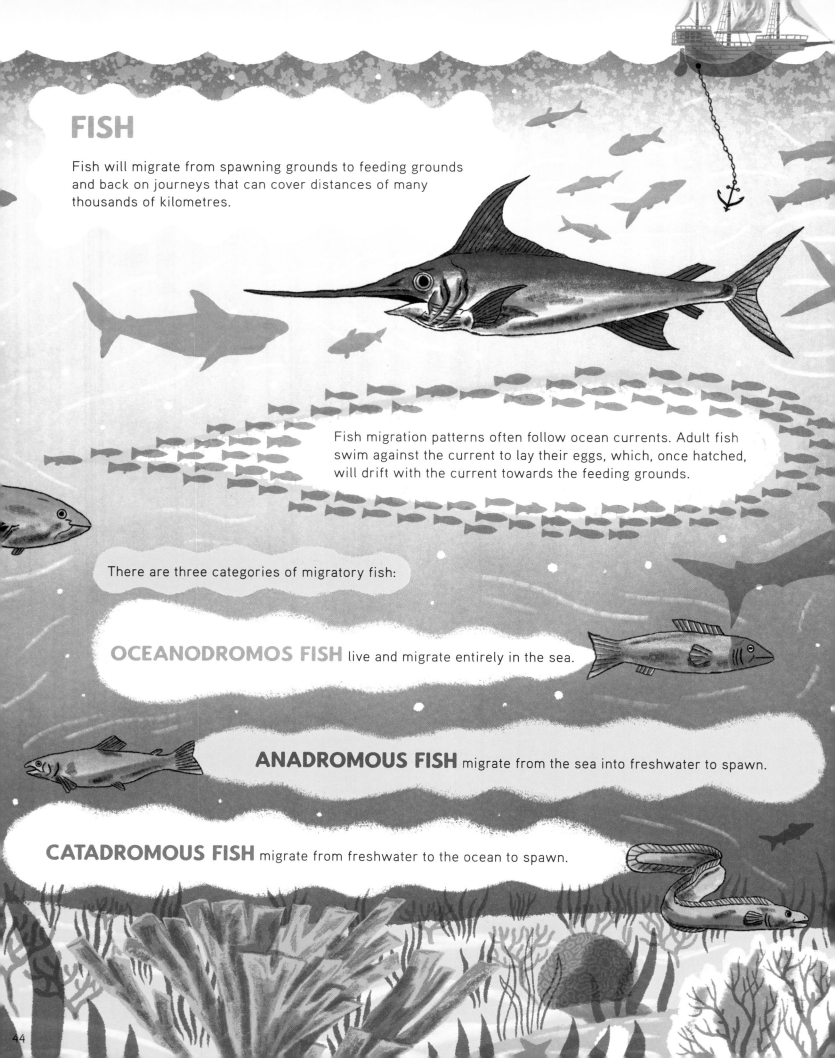

FISH

Fish will migrate from spawning grounds to feeding grounds and back on journeys that can cover distances of many thousands of kilometres.

Fish migration patterns often follow ocean currents. Adult fish swim against the current to lay their eggs, which, once hatched, will drift with the current towards the feeding grounds.

There are three categories of migratory fish:

OCEANODROMOS FISH live and migrate entirely in the sea.

ANADROMOUS FISH migrate from the sea into freshwater to spawn.

CATADROMOUS FISH migrate from freshwater to the ocean to spawn.

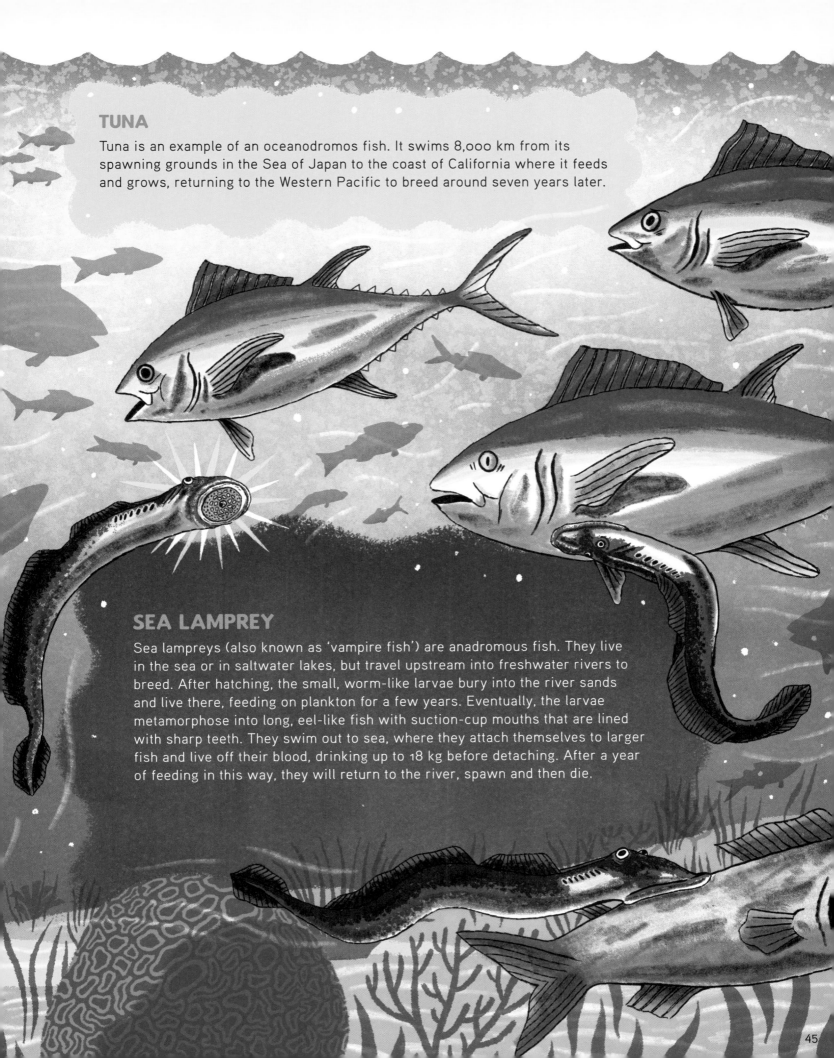

TUNA

Tuna is an example of an oceanodromos fish. It swims 8,000 km from its spawning grounds in the Sea of Japan to the coast of California where it feeds and grows, returning to the Western Pacific to breed around seven years later.

SEA LAMPREY

Sea lampreys (also known as 'vampire fish') are anadromous fish. They live in the sea or in saltwater lakes, but travel upstream into freshwater rivers to breed. After hatching, the small, worm-like larvae bury into the river sands and live there, feeding on plankton for a few years. Eventually, the larvae metamorphose into long, eel-like fish with suction-cup mouths that are lined with sharp teeth. They swim out to sea, where they attach themselves to larger fish and live off their blood, drinking up to 18 kg before detaching. After a year of feeding in this way, they will return to the river, spawn and then die.

SALMON

Salmon are another example of an anadromous fish, swimming from the sea upstream to freshwater rivers to lay their eggs.

When the eggs hatch, the baby salmon (called fry) drift downstream. After a year or two of living in the rivers, the fry metamorphose; their gills adapt to saltwater and their sides become silvery. They then set off on a journey of thousands of kilometres into their ocean feeding grounds.

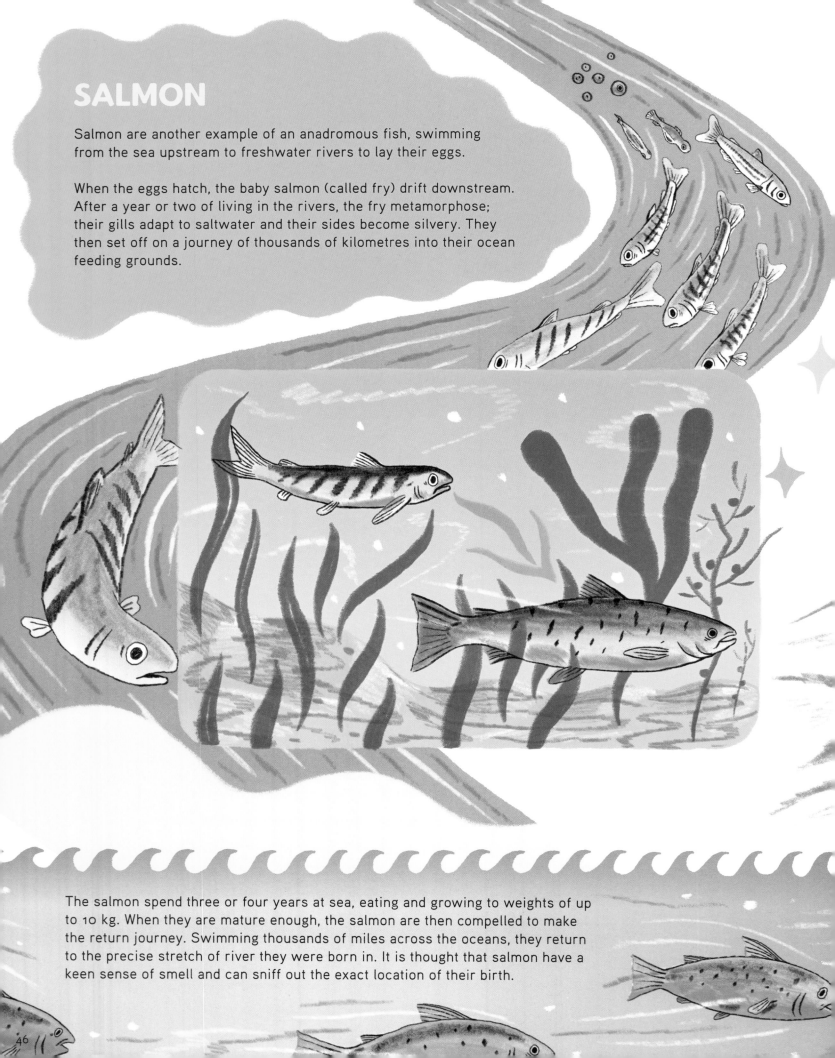

The salmon spend three or four years at sea, eating and growing to weights of up to 10 kg. When they are mature enough, the salmon are then compelled to make the return journey. Swimming thousands of miles across the oceans, they return to the precise stretch of river they were born in. It is thought that salmon have a keen sense of smell and can sniff out the exact location of their birth.

The journey takes an enormous amount of effort. The salmon will swim distances of more than 2,500 km to reach the river, and then hurl their powerful bodies upstream. They will stop at nothing to reach their destination, flinging themselves over boulders, waterfalls and any other obstacles in their path. If a river has been dammed, humans must install fish ladders to help the salmon get past.

This takes a terrible toll on the fish. The adult salmon's body is not suited to freshwater, and there is not much available food. They must absorb parts of their skeleton to fuel the brutal journey. Once the salmon have spawned, most of them deteriorate rapidly and die. These deteriorating salmon are called 'zombie fish'. Predators such as bears and eagles gather at the spawning sites to feast on the dying fish.

95% of salmon will die after spawning. However, a small proportion of fish will survive the ordeal, swimming back out to the ocean, where they will live until the time comes to repeat the entire journey and spawn again. These hardened veterans are called kelts.

EUROPEAN EELS

European eels are catadromous fish, meaning they live in freshwater and spawn in the sea. They have one of the most unusual lifecycles in the animal world, metamorphosing four times in their long lifespan.

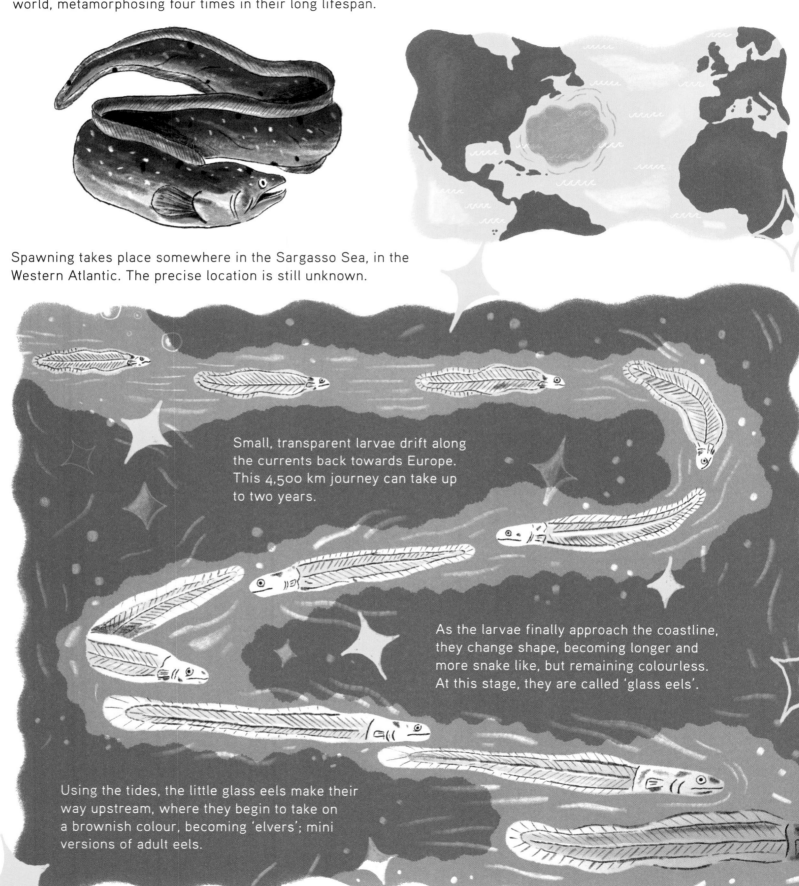

Spawning takes place somewhere in the Sargasso Sea, in the Western Atlantic. The precise location is still unknown.

Small, transparent larvae drift along the currents back towards Europe. This 4,500 km journey can take up to two years.

As the larvae finally approach the coastline, they change shape, becoming longer and more snake like, but remaining colourless. At this stage, they are called 'glass eels'.

Using the tides, the little glass eels make their way upstream, where they begin to take on a brownish colour, becoming 'elvers'; mini versions of adult eels.

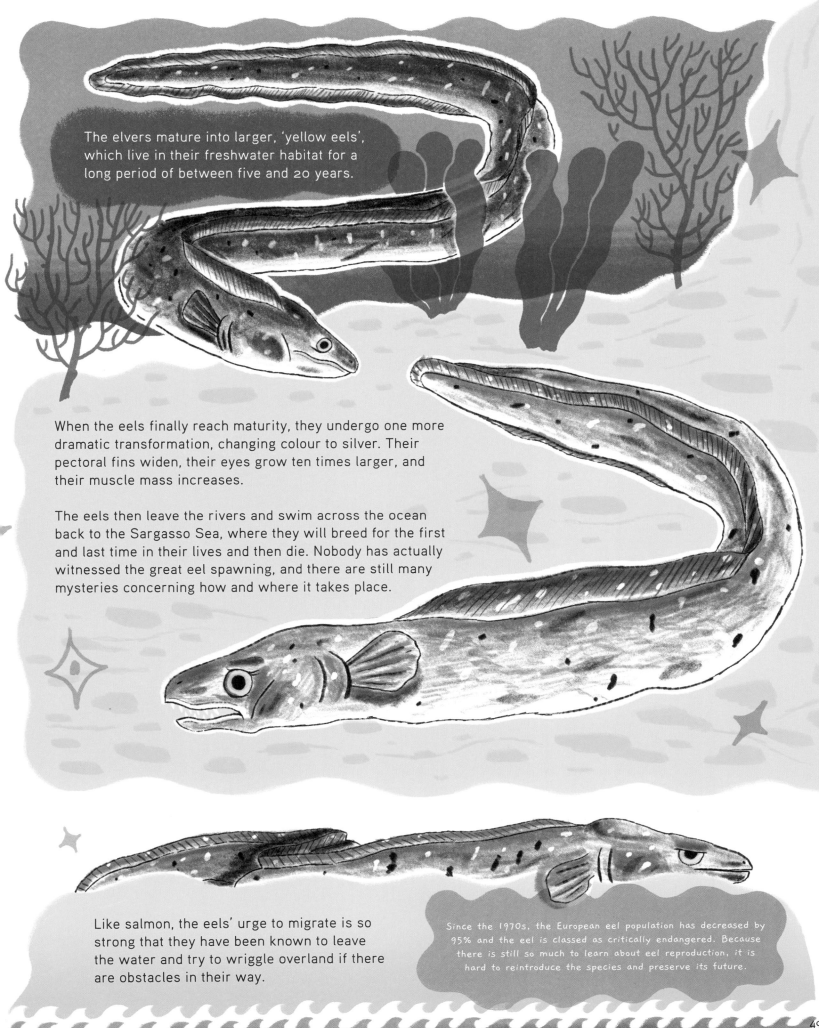

The elvers mature into larger, 'yellow eels', which live in their freshwater habitat for a long period of between five and 20 years.

When the eels finally reach maturity, they undergo one more dramatic transformation, changing colour to silver. Their pectoral fins widen, their eyes grow ten times larger, and their muscle mass increases.

The eels then leave the rivers and swim across the ocean back to the Sargasso Sea, where they will breed for the first and last time in their lives and then die. Nobody has actually witnessed the great eel spawning, and there are still many mysteries concerning how and where it takes place.

Like salmon, the eels' urge to migrate is so strong that they have been known to leave the water and try to wriggle overland if there are obstacles in their way.

Since the 1970s, the European eel population has decreased by 95% and the eel is classed as critically endangered. Because there is still so much to learn about eel reproduction, it is hard to reintroduce the species and preserve its future.

DIEL VERTICAL MIGRATION

The largest animal migration on the planet happens every single day. It is a journey from the depths of the ocean to the surface waters, and it is undertaken every nightfall by trillions of animals. It is called the diel vertical migration, or DVM.

Zooplankton are a group of mostly microscopic marine animals that live at the bottom of the ocean, at depths of 1,000 m and more. They feed on microscopic marine plants, called phytoplankton, which grow on the surface of the ocean. Zooplankton are delicious snacks for many fish, so they must hide in the murky depths during daylight hours, to avoid predators. As the sun sets, they undertake the kilometre-long journey to the surface; an impressive distance for such tiny creatures.

Small fish and squid will also undertake DVM, joining the zooplankton in their efforts to avoid predators.

As the earth rotates, wave upon wave of DVM can be seen swimming upwards. Before sunrise, they make the journey back down to the ocean deep.

DVM performs a useful function for the planet. Phytoplankton absorb a lot of CO_2 in the atmosphere. By eating the phytoplankton and taking the CO_2 back down to the depths of the ocean, DVM is an important way of keeping the earth's carbon levels in check.

LEATHERBACK TURTLES

Sea mammals and reptiles also undertake great migrations. The leatherback sea turtle is one of the most seasoned ocean travellers. Following the currents in search of delicious jellyfish, they journey as many as 17,000 km each year and then return to breed on the beaches they were born on.

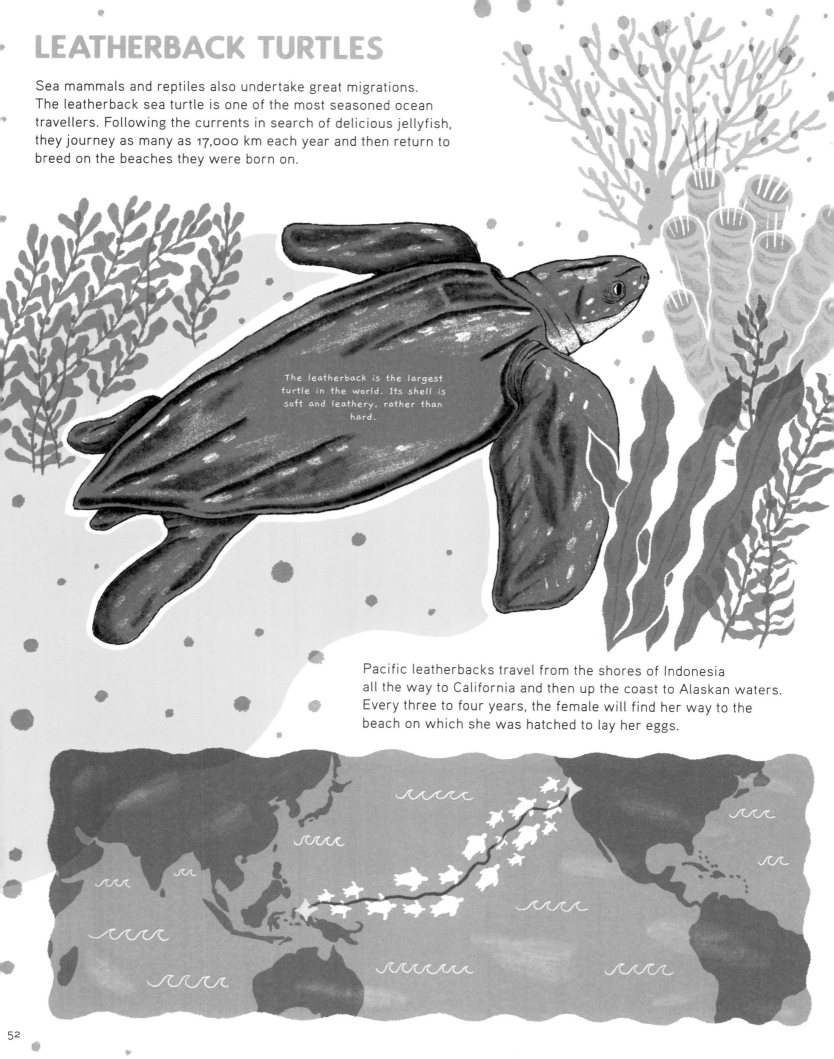

The leatherback is the largest turtle in the world. Its shell is soft and leathery, rather than hard.

Pacific leatherbacks travel from the shores of Indonesia all the way to California and then up the coast to Alaskan waters. Every three to four years, the female will find her way to the beach on which she was hatched to lay her eggs.

Over the course of 12 days, she will dig three or four pits in the sand with her flippers and lay over 100 eggs in each one.

When the eggs hatch 56 days later, the babies make their own migration. They dig their way out of the sand and follow the light of the moon to the sea. Predators lie in wait on the shore to snap them up. If there are artificial lights in the area, hatchlings will often head towards them rather than towards the sea. Fewer than three percent of the hatchlings will reach adulthood.

The leatherback has a pink spot on top of its head. Scientists think that this allows light to reach the part of the brain that is responsible for migration, signalling when the season for breeding has arrived.

WHALES

Many species of whales migrate from their breeding grounds to their feeding grounds and back, covering many thousands of miles a year. Some whales migrate north to south, some move between shallower waters and the deep ocean and some do both.

Baleen whales, such as grey whales, humpback whales and blue whales feed on tiny marine creatures called plankton. Instead of teeth, they have a giant, bristly mouth-sieve, called a baleen, which filters the plankton from the seawater into their mouths.

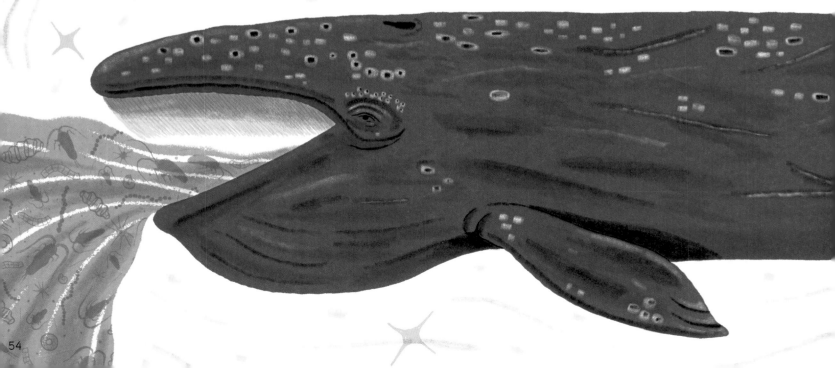

These whales follow the plankton to the waters of the Arctic and Antarctic, feeding non-stop and building up a thick layer of fat called blubber. In the autumn, the whales migrate to warmer waters in the tropics and sub-tropics to give birth. Their calves would not survive in polar waters without an insulating layer of blubber, so they must give them time grow and develop before they can embark on the return journey.

Whale milk is extremely high in fat, helping the baby whales build up blubber. Blue whale mothers can produce 200 litres of milk a day with a fat content of 50%!

Of these whales, grey whales are thought to have the longest migrations, travelling a distance of around 20,000 km round trip. Shipping and fishing industries can make this journey perilous, and many species of whales are now endangered.

Navigating Change

We humans rely on tools to help us locate ourselves; we need a compass, a map or satellite navigation to take us from A to B. If we were dropped into an unfamiliar landscape without these tools, most of us would find ourselves very lost indeed.

Migrating animals face no such problems. A homing pigeon will make a beeline to its nest no matter where in the world it is placed. A cuckoo is born without any cuckoo parents to lead the way, and yet within its first year of life, it unerringly makes its way to breeding grounds thousands of kilometres away.

Scientists still do not understand exactly how animals find their way across such vast distances so accurately. What we do know is that the complex balance of senses, instincts and learned behaviours do not take into account the impact that we humans have had upon the world. Light pollution, habitat loss and climate change are major disruptors of the delicate biological systems that tell animals when to breed, when to feed up and when to migrate. Animals must now navigate not just around the planet but also around the barriers that humans have placed in their way.

THE MYSTERIES OF NAVIGATION AND ORIENTATION

Animal navigators can cross the entire planet every year and never be thrown off course. As we have seen, an Arctic tern circumnavigates the globe in a single year, salmon find their way to the precise stretch of river they were born in, and monarch butterflies cross a continent to winter in specific trees in Mexico. So how do they do it?

This is a question that has boggled the human mind for thousands of years. 20,000 year-old cave paintings show land mammals migrating across the African savannah. The Ancient Greek philosopher, Aristotle, believed that birds morphed into different species in the winter. Two other theories that persisted until the 19th century were that migratory birds spent the winter hibernating in the mud at the bottom of lakes and that certain birds grew like fruit on trees! Although we now know these theories are incorrect, there are still many questions surrounding animal navigation.

Bats orient themselves by emitting high-pitched sounds and then listening for the echoes that are produced when the sound waves bounce off objects around them. This is called echolocation.

Using tools like banding, radar monitoring and tracking devices, scientists are gaining valuable insights into migration habits and routes and piecing together a picture of how it works. They have concluded that different species use different techniques to find their way home. Broadly, it seems that most migratory animals are able to sense the earth's magnetic field, registering roughly where on the planet they might be. They then use additional senses like sight, hearing and smell as well as echolocation ('seeing' with sound) and electroreception (detecting electric pulses) to pinpoint exactly how to get to their destination.

MAGNETIC MIGRANTS

The key to the incredible navigation skills of the world's most dramatic animal migrants seems to lie in the magnetic field that is generated by the earth's molten core. Many of the species that undertake the longest journeys (birds and sea creatures), appear to have an inbuilt compass that tells them where they are on the planet. This sixth sense is called magnetoreception.

Despite more than 50 years of research, scientists are unable to agree exactly where this inbuilt compass lies. Some scientists believe that the answer lies in a mineral called magnetite, which is found in bird beaks, fish noses and in the abdomens of honey bees. They believe that this mineral is very sensitive to magnetic fields, and can tell an animal not only which way it is heading but also what distance it is from the earth's poles.

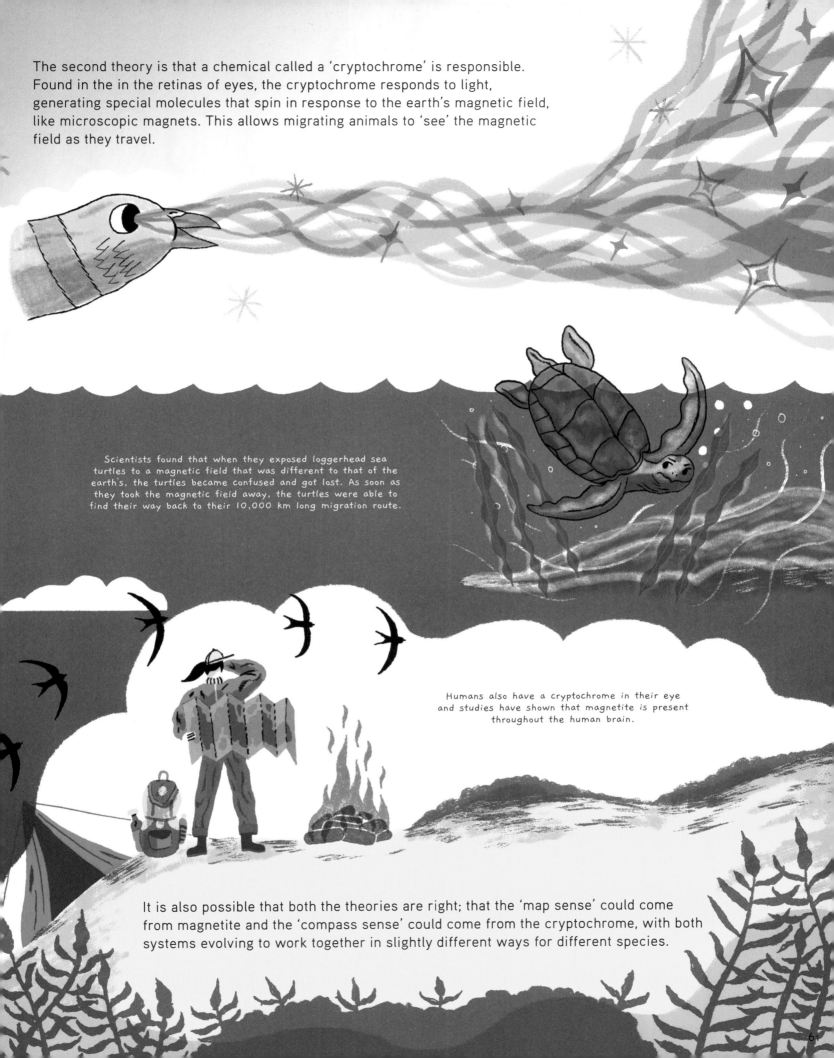

The second theory is that a chemical called a 'cryptochrome' is responsible. Found in the in the retinas of eyes, the cryptochrome responds to light, generating special molecules that spin in response to the earth's magnetic field, like microscopic magnets. This allows migrating animals to 'see' the magnetic field as they travel.

Scientists found that when they exposed loggerhead sea turtles to a magnetic field that was different to that of the earth's, the turtles became confused and got lost. As soon as they took the magnetic field away, the turtles were able to find their way back to their 10,000 km long migration route.

Humans also have a cryptochrome in their eye and studies have shown that magnetite is present throughout the human brain.

It is also possible that both the theories are right; that the 'map sense' could come from magnetite and the 'compass sense' could come from the cryptochrome, with both systems evolving to work together in slightly different ways for different species.

The earth's magnetic field is important for the long-distance phase of migration, but as the animals get closer to their destination, they enter the homing in phase, in which each species will use different methods to sense precisely where they need to go.

Familiar landmarks can serve as important homing devices. Topographical landmarks, like rivers and coastlines, ecological indicators like vegetation zones, and climate landmarks like air pressure and humidity can all point the animals in the right direction. Experiments in a planetarium proved that night-flying birds use the stars to navigate. When the constellations were shifted slightly, the birds lost their bearings.

Homing pigeons are excellent navigators, finding their way back to their nests from many hundreds of miles away. In one experiment, scientists found that pigeons that were deprived of their sense of smell struggled to find their nests. They concluded that pigeons see the landscape beneath them as a 'smell map', with their nest as a big, fragrant signpost. Salmon are also experts at smelling, detecting the changing mineral content in seas and rivers to find their way to their spawning grounds.

Other species use more mysterious cues to pinpoint their homes. Whales and giraffes listen out for low-frequency soundwaves called infrasound. Eels and sharks can navigate by sensing electric fields underwater, and many insects are able to make use of polarized light patterns, which are formed when light is scattered by airborne particles. This helps them locate where the sun is coming from, even on cloudy days.

OTHER FACTORS

Scientists believe that in many cases, migration routes are inherited genetically. Young birds who have been raised in captivity will find their way to the migration routes of their species without being taught what those routes are. However, many species teach their young how to fine-tune their journeys.

Studies of whooping cranes found that young birds that travelled with their elders for a few years improved the efficiency of their journeys by up to 20%, taking more direct routes and making the most of thermal currents.

Communication can also play into the fine tuning of migration routes. Animals that travel in flocks, schools or herds will 'talk' to one another to make sure that the group is staying together on the right migration path, away predators and other hazards. Whales will sing, telling each other where they have come from and where they are headed.

The great diel vertical migration (see p. 52) has been known to emit a sound that works as a kind of 'dinner bell' telling the huge community of zooplankton that it's time to rise up from the depths of the ocean to its surface to feed.

Environmental factors, like wind thermals and ocean currents, also play a role in migration routes. Fish will swim against the current to reach their breeding grounds so that the eggs and larvae can drift passively with the ocean currents to the feeding grounds where they will mature.

Humans too were once expert navigators. Polynesians effortlessly crossed thousands of miles of open sea to reach small inhabited islands. An experiment found that humans with real magnets attached to their heads cannot point in the direction of home nearly as well as those with fake magnets, indicating that somewhere deep inside we too may have or once had a navigation sense.

MIGRATION IN A CHANGING WORLD

Climate change is affecting the habitats of all animals in the world, but migrating species are particularly vulnerable, as they rely not on one ecosystem, but several. For example, it's not just the breeding and feeding grounds of migrating birds that are important, but every resting point and every thermal current along the way.

Scientists are finding that, due to warming temperatures, birds are laying eggs earlier in the year, meaning that their young are vulnerable to predators, parasites and diseases that would not normally be found in colder climates. When the birds fly south for the winter, their once lush winter homes are often parched and desert-like.

The situation is made worse by the degradation of land by overuse, logging, urbanisation and farming. Land mammals struggle to follow the rains across big roads and around man-made obstacles. Land bridges have been constructed in some instances to help the animals move freely.

There is a long list of further problems caused by humans. Wetlands that were once important stopping points for migrating shorebirds have been drained and developed. Artificial lighting and pollution can disrupt the navigational abilities of birds, reptiles and insects. Warming oceans mean that fish species are struggling to adapt, and plastics in the ecosystem can disrupt the release of hormones that tell the animals when to migrate and when to breed.

Scientists continue to learn how migration works and how the ecosystems of the planet rely on one another. With knowledge comes power and responsibility; The more we understand, the more we are able to protect the animals that share this amazing planet that we all call home.

GLOSSARY

Anadromous fish   Fish that migrate from the sea into freshwater to spawn.

Artiodactyla   A family of large grazing mammals with cloven (split) hooves.

Bounding flight   Small migratory birds fly in a 'bouncing' pattern – they flap a few times, then close their wings and glide for short periods.

Catadromous fish   Fish that migrate from freshwater to the ocean to spawn.

Cryptochrome   A chemical found in the retina of some animals' eyes that allows them to 'see' the magnetic field of the earth.

Diel vertical migration (DVM)   The journey of billions of microscopic marine animals from the depths of the ocean to its surface to feed on phytoplankton. It happens every sunset and sunrise in oceans throughout the world.

Echolocation   A sense which allows animals like bats and dolphins orient themselves by emitting high-pitched sounds and listening to the reverberations.

Electroreception   A sense in which animals orient themselves by detecting electrical pulses within the water.

Flapping flight   Birds with shorter wings flap, rather than glide. This uses more energy but gives them more flexibility, allowing them to fly at high altitudes, to fly at night and to take direct routes to their destination.

Flyways   Regular flight paths that species of birds follow year on year.

Gliding flight   Birds with small bodies and large wings make the most of thermal currents to glide for long distances without flapping, saving over 75% of their energy, and allowing them to make quicker journeys without spending time refuelling.

Kelts   Salmon that survive their arduous spawning migration and make it back to the ocean to spawn again.

Leapfrog migration Some birds of the same species have longer migrations than others. Geese from the most northerly populations will fly to the most southerly destinations, meaning that their migration route is many times longer than that of geese from southerly populations.

Loop migration When birds return to their nesting grounds via a different migration route.

Magnetite A mineral found in the beaks of birds and the noses of fish that may act as a tiny compass, helping animals orient themselves within the earth's magnetic field.

Magnetoreception The ability present in many migratory animals that allows them to sense the earth's magnetic field and orient themselves within it.

Nomadic migration When animals travel a short distance every day throughout the year, rather than embarking on long migrations seasonally.

Oceanodromos fish Fish that live and migrate entirely in the sea.

Phytoplankton Microscopic marine plants that live on the surface of the water and absorb CO_2.

Polymorphic insects When insects of the same species have different body types depending on whether they are responsible for mating or migration.

Ringing When researchers put a metal band on a bird's leg so that they may identify it and track its journey.

Stopover sites Areas where many birds gather to rest and refuel on their migration route.

Thermal current Columns of warm air that spiral upwards, allowing broad-winged birds to glide for many miles without flapping.

V-formation A flight formation in which birds reduce the air resistance by sheltering behind the bird in front. The bird at the front of the 'V' will be doing the hardest work, and the birds will rotate to take turns at the front.

Zooplankton Microscopic marine animals that feed on microscopic marine plants.

ANIMAL INDEX

For Bob and Maribel, the Browns, the Edwards, the Davidsons
and Jem. Thank you for everything, I love you all.
Thanks also to Ziggy Hanaor at Cicada for the support.
-- EB

Epic Animal Journeys

Text © Ed J Brown and Ziggy Hanaor
Illustration © Ed J Brown
www.edjbrown.com

British Library Cataloguing-in-Publication Data.

A CIP record for this book is available from the British Library
ISBN: 978-1-80066-029-8

First published in 2022 in the UK, 2023 in the USA

Cicada Books Ltd
48 Burghley Road
London, NW5 1UE
www.cicadabooks.co.uk

Printed in Poland on FSC® certified paper.